Requests for permission to reproduce parts of this work should be addressed to the author. Contact information can be found on the author's website:

www.ordinarydudemeditation.com

If you would like to invite the author to speak at an event for your organization or are interested in his personal development services, please contact him via the website.

To my mom and dad,

who instilled in me the belief that anything is possible.

TABLE OF CONTENTS

Introduction:

How habits can be fun, simple, and life-changing

If you're reading this book, you've probably tried to change your habits.

You've likely set out on ambitious new year's resolutions, tried to kick a couple bad habits, or start a promising new routine. My guess is you picked up this book because you're an ordinary dude who has failed at changing habits one too many times.

You may wonder why it is that, year after year, you're stuck in the same place? Still not exercising, still eating junk food every day, still with less than a hundred dollars saved, and still asking yourself why nothing changes. It probably feels somewhat defeating.

You may have given up on habit change altogether, but I want to tell you there's still hope. You just need to know where to start.

Many of the habit books out there probably seem far too scientific, heady, or boring to read. "Boringness" is a key reason many ordinary dudes struggle. But it's not the only one. There are three reasons us dudes give up on habit change.

1. Habit change isn't fun

Imagine being someone else for a day…

Instead of the dude you are, who has done things a certain way for years and is comfortably set in a routine, you get to be a new person.

- If you feel sluggish most days…what if you could be a dude who felt light, lean, and full of energy?

- If you feel endlessly anxious…what if you could experience what it's like to be regularly calm and centered?

- If you feel hopeless often…what if you could be in control of your life, ready to take on the world?

If you ask me, experiencing what it's like to be a different person sounds pretty fun. And that's exactly what habit change can do for you.

In fact, changing dozens of habits has enabled me to experience many lives. Habit change has helped me feel less foggy-headed and see the world in brighter colors (when I limited booze and caffeine); kick my anxiety (meditation); and look and feel as fit as I was in my late teens and early 20s (exercising two to four times a week). And even the times when I decided not to stick with a habit, it gave me a glimpse into another lifestyle—opening a window to another world that could be mine if I wanted.

When I gave up Facebook for 40 days, I was amazed how less distracted I felt. When I quit reading the news for a month, I suddenly no longer felt irritated by headlines that made it seem like the world was ending. When I stopped drinking soda for two months, I felt less anxious and sludgy, and a bit calmer. I returned to all these habits for different reasons, but it did show me what life could be like without them. And experimenting with your habits can do the same for you.

I won't lie, the tactics you implement to change a habit aren't exactly fun. But the different lives you'll experience, some within just a week of starting your habit, will be pretty exciting. You'll likely find that testing out a new lifestyle is well worth your time.

2. Habit change is too difficult

It's easy to overwhelm yourself when thinking about changing a habit. Thinking about all the effort that's involved week after week can feel like an insurmountable force. Take exercise for example. In my experience, it takes several months of effort to create a lasting exercise habit. That's a long time. And if you dwell on the long and difficult road, you can get discouraged.

The strategies I'll discuss in this book break it down nice and simple for you. Instead of thinking about all the effort it takes to change, we'll focus on baby steps. The easy tactics you can start now that reduce effort. Instead of focusing on the staircase (the effort and long road to habit change), we're going to focus on the steps. And you'll soon see, it's going to become a whole lot easier.

3. Habit change doesn't matter

When you're comfortable with your current habits, what does it really matter if you give up?

Truthfully, it doesn't matter much in the short term. But the habits you create today can have a dramatic effect on your life in the long term. Darren Hardy's book *The Compound Effect* explains this brilliantly.

Hardy uses investing as a metaphor. Investing a couple hundred bucks a month makes little difference in the short term, but compounded over 30 years that money suddenly turns into hundreds of thousands, or even millions of dollars. It is the same with habits as well. Reaching for that daily bag of chips has little effect today, or next week. But if you repeat that habit over several years, you'll likely find yourself overweight and with health problems. You may see few results in a week or two when starting a swimming routine, but after years of doing it, your health and physique will be way better than many of your friends.

Looking at the big picture is one of the keys to habit change, which I'll explain in more detail later in the book.

No matter the reason you struggle with habits, it's easy to push aside a new routine or change...especially when the next episode of *Game of Thrones* is on, your buddies await you at the bar, or the couch is calling you for a nap. But the rewards of changing a habit are absolutely incredible. My habits have enabled me to publish three books, start work on two more, feel more energized, save close to $20,000 in a few short years, and accomplish many of my personal goals. Whatever your ambition is, the result is the goal, the habits are the path to success.

What's more, changing your habits will make you feel good about yourself. By changing even a small habit, like waking up a half hour earlier for example, you will begin to feel more and more confident. Like you can accomplish anything. And the truth is, you can.

For the ordinary dude, habit change can be confusing. But it doesn't have to be. Like all *Ordinary Dude Guides*, this one offers the same type of goodies: provides you practical, easy-to-follow steps to make a change. In this book that change is all about habits.

I originally wrote this book to complement *An Ordinary Dude's Guide to Meditation*. I always tell people, meditation is easy. The hard part is forming the habit. While I do mention tactics I used to start meditating, this book is about much more than meditation. It's about ordinary habits us dudes struggle with—like exercising regularly, quitting smoking, saving money, eating healthier, reading more, or breaking a smartphone addiction, among others.

Over the years, I've changed dozens of habits. I started a flossing habit in my late teens, quit smoking in my mid 20s, started meditating again every day when I was 30, and many others. But, out of any year in my life, I've never changed as many habits as I did in 2017. Over the course of that year, I changed eight habits in total. Some as easy as making my bed every morning to more difficult habits like cutting my alcohol and coffee consumption down to a few days a week. I also changed some habits that are quite typical. Some that many an ordinary dude would like to change him or herself. Exercising every week and saving a couple hundred dollars every month are some of the more commonly desired habits I conquered. Saving $300 a month was rather easy, as it's a habit I established before. The alcohol, coffee and exercise habits, however, were exceptionally excruciating because I didn't understand their root cause. But I'll get into that more later.

With that said, we all learn from failure. And the lessons I learned from my early habit failures are the source of some practical tips you'll find throughout this book. So, shall we get down to it?

The first step to changing any habit is to examine why a change hasn't already happened.

Chapter 1

Why dudes fail at habit change

On my quest to change dozens of habits, I've identified three prime causes of failure. I believe all dudes, myself included, struggle with these at one point or another. We'll go through each of them in this chapter, starting with one of biggest reasons many dudes quit on habit change (or any change for that matter): failure itself.

So let's start here.

1. Failure demotivates you

Failure is a bitter brew to swallow. Failing even once can leave you hopeless—sabotaging your chances of succeeding before you even start. Why bother with a diet, an exercise routine, or quitting smoking when you've already failed once?

"Surely, I'll fail again," you may think. So you might as well do nothing and resign yourself to your bad habits.

The truth is, all of us have some fear of failure. Even after failing thousands of times in my own life, a new failure still stings. But it's possible to fail once, and then succeed on your second, tenth, or even fiftieth try. Before I successfully started my weekly exercise routine on January 1, 2017, I had failed a good dozen or so times. Before I quit smoking in my mid-20s, I failed on at least two dozen occasions prior.

And, of course, there are many historic and famous people who suffered failures. Thomas Edison failed a thousand times on his quest to invent the lightbulb[1]. Stephen King's first novel, *Carrie*, was rejected 30 times before it was finally published. Before the Disney empire conquered the globe, Walt attempted to start a film studio that eventually went bankrupt. Yes, even the Mickey Mouse dude failed, and there are countless more similar stories....

These revolutionaries and global influencers were just ordinary dudes, like you and me, but they pushed forward after each failure and eventually touched the lives of billions of people.

To successfully develop any new habit, you need to start. And fear of failure prevents many from doing just that. In my previous book, *An Ordinary Dude's Guide to Meditation*, I mentioned this, but it's worth repeating.

The six-year-old man

Have you ever heard of a six-year-old man? You know, a six-year-old who is as tall as a man, makes wise decisions like an old dude, and sips on wine while reading Aristotle?

Me neither.

For any six-year-old boy, the process of becoming a man doesn't happen overnight. The child must first go to school, learn how to stick up for and take care of himself, control his emotions, and live through countless failures. No one expects a six-year-old to act like a full-grown dude. People understand children need time to develop, grow, and learn from their experiences. Kids aren't born perfect. Failure is part of improving. So why should you expect anything different from yourself?

If you've failed at starting a diet once or twice, you may think it's impossible to ever get it right...but how many times did you fail at learning to read or ride a bike before achieving success? Once or twice? You know as well as I do that we failed at these activities dozens or even hundreds of times. And for you to start your new habit, you have to accept it's likely going to take more than one or two failures to achieve your goal.

In our society, there's a misconception that, once you're an adult, you've got it all figured out. The truth is, age is irrelevant. We never stop growing. So, like a child, go easy on yourself and accept you don't have a lot of experience in your new skill. But instead of naively believing you'll succeed quickly, know that more often than not you're going to shoot and miss.

Prepare yourself to fail

When you set out on your mission to instill a new habit, **expect setbacks**. This prevents you from feeling devastated when you fail. Of course, accepting failure is easier said than done. That's why you should prepare yourself for the inevitable feelings. Failure will sting like a bitch.

You'll feel frustrated, defeated, and ready to give up. You'll want to drown your sorrows in a beer and pizza. But don't avoid your feelings. When you're sad, just let those feelings be. Get a good rest, take a walk outside, or get some exercise. But do me a favor. Save the beer and the pizza for celebrations, for the good times. You'll find more solace talking to a friend than in stuffing your face. It may take a day or two, or even a week, but I promise you this: the feelings of failure will pass just like a thunderstorm does or pain from a scraped knee.

Failure is one of the many wounds that will heal. And when it does, it's time to reflect on what caused the failure, alter your behavior accordingly, and plough ahead with your habit change.

Will you fail every time you change a habit?

No, it's possible to succeed instantly. But this often depends on the difficulty of the habit you're changing. For example, I've habitually made my bed every day since July 2017—never failing once. But making your bed is easy; it takes just a minute or two. It's not as daunting of a challenge as exercising weekly or quitting smoking. You may never fail when changing a simple routine. But for everything else, expect setbacks.

Not preparing for failure is, of course, only one piece of the habit-change puzzle.

2. The small picture & the easy way out

"Just one candy bar...I swear...after that, I'm back on my diet. I promise."

If you've ever tried to lose weight or attempted to quit indulging in a favorite food or drink, these or similar words have surely crossed your mind. But please. Don't listen to the voice of temptation. If you hear yourself say, "Just this once, I promise..." go splash some cold water on your face and tell your buddy to slap you. You're about to cave on your new habit.

I know, it's difficult to make a change when the candy bar, pizza, cigarette, or donut is right there in your face. It's almost irresistible. And that's why you have to look at the big picture.

"But dude! That's easier said than done," you say.

It is. So let me tell you a story....

It may be hard to believe that a dude like myself—who has a deep love of stouts, blondes, porters, and ales of all kinds—has actually given up all beers, spirits, and alcohol for five-months straight. But that's exactly what I did in the summer of 2011. Why would a dude like myself do such a horrendous thing? It all started with an unrelenting case of athlete's foot. Yes, I know it's a bit gross, but bear with me.

If you're like most dudes, you may have caught a case of athlete's foot once or twice before. It's uncomfortable, itchy and, yes, embarrassing. My case of the foul fungus was caught in Australia and stuck with me for two years...two freakin' years! I tried creams and talked with doctors, but nothing seemed to get rid of the problem. So I did something extreme. I diverted from the standard medical treatment path and sought out a Chinese herbalist who suggested alcohol was fueling the condition.

God help me...

But the herbalist had a point. Every time I drank, my athlete's foot flared up.

As with anyone trying to restrict their diet, you can imagine I had my fair share of temptation. And I did. Especially since I visited bars regularly with friends during that five-month period. But I couldn't give in. The reason is, I kept my focus on the big picture.

I was tired of the nagging annoyance and embarrassment of athlete's foot. Every time I was tempted to have a drink, I thought about how badly I wanted to get rid of the fungus and move on with my life. I knew if I succumbed to the mindset of "just this once" and had even a single drink with my buddies, it could easily lead to two, three, or ten more that week. If I didn't look past the small picture—past the stein on the table with the golden glow, past my time at the bar and into the future, to the bigger picture— then I may have easily fallen to temptation.

And if you've ever attempted to restrict your diet, quit smoking or halt any addiction, you've surely been there. Tempted to give in **just this once**. Of course, it's difficult to resist. It's difficult to say "no" when giving in is so easy. And feeling this way is nothing to be ashamed of. We're all human.

That's why it's important to look at the big picture. Every time you look at, hear or smell your temptation, think about how you want your life to look in three months, one year, or a decade. What happens if you give in?

Let me tell you what you already know—you've been down that road. And this is your chance to choose a different path. No, it's not easy to sacrifice the short for the long term. So long term needs to be your focus. When temptation arises, change your focus from the impulse at hand to the image of your life you want to create. Literally imagine your life in the future.

If you can quit your bad habit, how will your life look in a year? How will you feel? Will you be happier or healthier? Will people act differently towards you?

This is your key to lasting change. And while focusing on the short term is just one cause of habit failure, we're not finished yet.

3. Information overload, chaotic times, and bad decisions' breeding ground

The information age comes with both good and bad. Yes, any information you desire can be yours. Thanks to our modern-day version of the oracle, Google, you can get answers to almost any question in mere seconds. Of course, there's a downside to all this, one that people seldom talk about: information overload.

From books, newspapers, and billions of web pages to TV and all the other forms of media, there's a mind-boggling array of information out there. You could surf the internet non-stop for the rest of your life and not consume even a fraction of it all.

With easy access to this information available via the smartphone in your pocket, it can become nearly impossible to think clearly. If you're like most people, your mind is constantly muddled with new stories, advice, song lyrics, gossip, random thoughts, and all sorts of other information. The problem is, how can you expect to change a habit when your mind is so cluttered?

Changing a habit is no doubt difficult. Typically it requires breaking a habit that's already cemented as part your daily routine and then repeating the new habit on a daily basis. Doing a task over and over again requires focus.

Focus is one of the most important elements of habit change. Changing any habit requires a strong, focused effort to set and then keep it in motion. Understand that the less you can focus, the less chance you have of changing.

An example from my own life.... I'm a big fan of setting goals at the start of each year. And from 2014 to 2016, I had a habit of creating a list of 30 to 60 goals to accomplish in the ensuing 12-month period. At the end of 2016, I realized in the previous years I'd done this, I only accomplished about half my goals— and not the ones most important to me. So for 2017, I decided to do something extreme. I gave myself just two goals to accomplish: exercise two to four times a week, for all 52 weeks, and earn four times as much money as I was at the beginning of 2017. These were lofty goals. I had failed at starting an exercise routine many times. And earning four times my current salary would be more money than I'd ever made in any of my four years in Bangkok.

Low and behold, by the end of 2017 I had managed to accomplish both. Focusing on only two goals, it was easy to remember what I was working towards every day as I made efforts to accomplish them. Remembering 30 to 60 goals off the top of my head was impossible. But two was simple. The reduced number of goals kept me focused, which leads me to a valuable lesson...

Less focus = less change

A big reason I recommend meditation is because it helps you develop the ability to focus for long periods. The more you can focus, the more you'll be able to accomplish anything you want. But focus has enemies that are bigger than the billions of distractions and heaps of information out there.

If Focus were a superdude, Chaos would be a badass villain

You've likely experienced a time of personal crisis. Maybe your world was turned upside down by a friend or family member's death, a huge financial hit, or a job loss. Either way, a personal crisis is one example of when chaos creeps into your life. However, chaos comes in many forms.

And it's not just the bad, good times can be equally chaotic. A pregnancy or birth of a child can throw your world into disarray. A new job or a flood of work can make other parts of your life, other goals, fall to the wayside.

Chaos, good or bad, can destroy any chance of starting a habit. When times are turbulent, the willpower to stay focused and push forward often gives out, and we settle for microwavable dinners, booze, and succumbing to the allure of delivery pizza and Netflix. The easy way out is just far too appealing.

So what can you do to avoid the roadblock of chaos? Simply be aware of it. If you're trying to start a habit during a big life change or personal crisis, know your chances of failure have probably quadrupled. It may be best to wait out the turbulence. Does that mean it's impossible to change habits during chaotic times? Absolutely not.

I started and changed a total of eight habits in 2017 and it was one of the most turbulent years of my life. We'll get into the nuts and bolts of how I did this later. But for now, just realize chaos is a major cause of habit failure.

---

[1] Well, dude. Complete transparency, it appears there's quite a debate about the number of Edison's failed attempts at the lightbulb. 1,000 seems like a popular number, but as the following article explains, the real answer is uncertain. Let's just say he failed a lot.

http://www.nightingale.com/newsletters/556 See full citation in Endnotes.

Chapter 2

Habit myths

Habit change isn't always straightforward. Just like the three causes of failure mentioned in the last chapter, believing myths can derail your efforts.

Most of the following four strategies are widely accepted. And in this chapter, we'll examine each one, as well as tactics to sidestep the hidden stumbling blocks. Let's start with the granddaddy of all habit change beliefs—that all you need is willpower.

Myth 1: Self-discipline can conquer any habit

There's a common belief that willpower is enough to change a habit. Instead of coming up with a strategy, you rely on self-discipline. You suck it up and force the habit change.

Many people are familiar with this mindset. Maybe you're determined to stamp out a pesky habit after reading an inspiring book, having a good week, or some other confidence booster. Now, you're going to assert your will and get er' done.

Truth be told, all habit change tactics require some willpower. But relying on willpower alone is a recipe for failure. We don't have an unlimited supply. It can be worn down and, once it's depleted, you're left vulnerable to the alluring comfort of old habits. Want some evidence?

Consider this 1996 study by Roy Baumeister.

A group of college students were asked to participate in a supposed "food perception" test. They were asked not to eat for three hours before coming to the lab. When the students got there, they were greeted with the delightful smell of fresh baked cookies and two bowls on a table: one filled with chocolate chip cookies and another with radishes. The researchers explained that these two foods were chosen because of their distinctive tastes, and the participants would be contacted tomorrow to discuss their thoughts on the taste sensations.

Half the participants were lucky. They were instructed to eat two or three chocolate chip cookies and no radishes. The other half were told to eat two or three radishes and no cookies. The researchers left the room and the participants ate.

Perhaps somewhat surprisingly, none of the radish eaters gave into temptation and snuck a single cookie. Willpower won out. As for the cookie eaters, surely they had no problem resisting the radishes, needing not use any willpower. Now, here's where things got interesting.

A second group of researchers entered the room to lead a supposedly unrelated study: to learn who was better at solving problems, college students or high school students. The study was framed this way to feed into the college students' egos. Certainly they'd be motivated to prove they were smarter than high schoolers.

So the college students were presented with a series of unsolvable puzzles. Of course, they didn't know the puzzles were unsolvable. The researchers wanted to see how long the students would keep trying before giving up. How did they do? The chocolate chip cookie group made 34 attempts at solving the puzzle over 19 minutes. The radish resistance, however, only managed 19 attempts over eight minutes. What caused the dramatic difference in effort?

The radish group ran out of willpower. It was depleted from resisting the chocolate chip cookies in the previous experiment. So, should it be so surprising that willpower is exhaustible?

Well, willpower in its essence is just effort—used to push forward or resist. It works similarly to exercise. Before your workout, you're fresh and ready. But once you start and then sweat, your energy levels diminish. Eventually you can no longer exert any more effort. You're spent. So it is with willpower as well.

For over a decade, I was a big believer in self-discipline. What I didn't realize is that when I thought I was solely relying on willpower, I was often using other strategies like replacement and long-term focus, which we'll get to later. I just wasn't conscious of the strategies yet, as I was still unfamiliar with them. With that said, in the past year I've come across another tactic that's an effective alternative to willpower.

Alter your environment to use less willpower

The foods you eat, the people you hang out with, the items in your house or fridge...all these things influence your behavior. So if you want to change your habits, consider altering your environment.

Food is a great example. If you're trying to lose weight, instead of buying a box of Little Debbies every week and then limiting yourself to one per day, just don't buy the box. Remove the temptation, and then you'll be less inclined to give in. Yes, you could still drive to the store and buy some Oatmeal Cream Pies, but that would require effort. Whereas in the study above where effort was used to resist, in this instance effort would need to be exerted. And let's face it, many of us dudes are lazy (myself included).

In Bangkok I often choose not to go to a particular store or even buy pizza because I have to cross the street. It's too much effort. That's because the streets here are freakin' chaotic and if you don't pay attention, it's quite easy to get hit. Thank god there's no Dairy Queen or pizzeria on my side of the street, or else I'd probably be ten pounds heavier. But I digress….

The point is, use effort to your advantage. If you're trying to quit Little Debbie, make it involve some effort to get her. It's true that if she's removed from your pantries, you probably won't get her chocolatey goodness out of your head immediately. But as time passes, you'll likely forget about her completely. Maybe you'll even replace her with a better suitor for your weight loss efforts, like the Chiquita banana lady.

Food isn't the only example. If you're trying to complain less, hang around with dudes who aren't complainers. The people you surround yourself with have a tremendous impact on your behavior. I've seen my behavior influenced both negatively and positively by those I spend time with. And I've seen my friends' behavior changed by a new girlfriend, boss, or drinking buddy.

The same goes for your direct environment. If you want to do any kind of task on a regular basis—such as reading, writing, or studying—then change your environment so it's optimal for that behavior. If you want to write for two hours, remove distractions from your environment, such as your phone, TV, or internet connection. Clean up the area where you'll be performing this task so you won't be distracted by clutter.

By removing distractions, temptations, and people who habitually do the behavior you want to avoid, it will be much easier to change your habit. You'll have to use less willpower. In other words, working harder then requires less discipline.

Prepare for chaotic times

Remember in Chapter 1 where I mentioned chaotic times were one of the main causes of habit failure? Well, if you alter your environment during chaotic times, there's less chance your new habit will be disrupted.

Suffer a personal crisis as you're trying to break a smartphone addiction? Well, if you ask your lady or guy to hide your smartphone once you arrive home, you're less likely to succumb to its temptation. And the chances of sticking with your habit increase.

Bear in mind, it's not a given you'll automatically change your habit by altering your environment. I still recommend implementing some of the many tactics in the next few chapters. Altering your environment will, however, make the process a hell of a lot easier.

Myth 2: Accountability—Tell everyone about your habit and you'll be pressured to succeed

Pick up almost any book on habit, and the author usually recommends accountability. The general idea is, tell everyone about your new habit and you'll feel embarrassed if you don't follow through. The result is you force yourself to change. With that said, I very seldom use accountability with habits. I've told the world about my habit changes on many occasions and failed more times than I can count. I've also seen my friends suffer the same fate using accountability. Why is this?

My thoughts are people initially get a natural high from telling everyone about their new habit. Change is exciting. Especially when friends and family give words of encouragement, like "way to go" and "you can do it, dude!" But when that encouragement disappears, so does the habit change. In other words, you get positive reinforcement for attempting a habit change, not completing one. There is a difference.

Quitting smoking is one the most common scenarios where this pattern plays out. Now, quitting smoking is probably one of the most difficult habits to change. When I was kicking smoking ten years ago, I fell into the habit of "getting rewarded" for attempting to quit.

I'd feel determined. Tell everyone, and then as I made it to day seven or day 10 without a cigarette, my pride would swell and I'd proclaim my accomplishment to even more friends. But then, maybe on day 15, when I told no one about quitting,

I'd slip. I smoked a cigarette. Sooner than you know, I was back to a half pack a day.

I saw this problem play out in my own life and have seen it happen to many friends over the years. For this reason, I rarely tell anyone I'm changing a habit these days. By doing this, I remind myself I'm not changing my habit for anyone but myself. The main purpose of your habit change is not to impress your friends or family, but to make your life better. Whether someone knows is irrelevant.

Once you've been performing your habit for several months, you likely won't even need to tell people you made the change. They'll just notice on their own. For example, I sometimes get compliments on my more toned physique as a result of my swimming habit. I never had to tell my friends that I was swimming on a regular basis; they just ask about what I'm doing, and I tell them I swim regularly.

With all that said, can accountability work? Sure. But there needs to be something on the line, and more involved than just telling everyone you know.

What does it really mean to be accountable?

Accountability is more effective when taken to extreme measures. In most scenarios I've heard where accountability works, the person who was attempting to change had something to lose. Literally. Posting on social media that you're changing typically isn't enough. There needs to be money on the line or some kind of consequence for failure.

For example, you could tell your best friend that if you fail to change your habit, he must post a naked picture of you online. Give him the picture before starting so you can't change your mind later. Now, I'll admit, posting nude photos of yourself online is extreme. In fact, I wouldn't ever recommend it; I just want to demonstrate the level of accountability needed. With that said, a similar type of method can work.

Instead of giving your best bud nude photos, which he probably doesn't want anyway, give him $500. If you fail, he donates that money to an organization or political campaign you despise. That way, it's a double sting for failure—you lose a lot of money and support something you hate.

Accountability does not always have to involve humiliation, or large donations to despicable organizations. I've seen accountability work first-hand in online communities. Many have had programs with accountability buddies. Essentially you team up with another dude who's also trying to change, and you support each other every step of the way.

I personally believe that accountability through a paid program works better than just with one of your buddies. There's money in the game. I've tried to hold friends accountable for habits before and seen it fail. There was no money involved. They had nothing to lose and, of course, as my friends, I'll still love them regardless of whether they maintain their new habit.

Another type of paid accountability is to hire a coach. As I mentioned earlier in this book, when I cut alcohol and sugar from my diet to cure athlete's foot, I saw a Chinese herbalist on a bi-weekly basis. I didn't know it at the time, but she acted as a coach to help me succeed. She was with me every step of the way providing support and advice. What's more, there was an added psychological incentive, as I didn't want to disappoint her or feel as though I was paying money for nothing.

So if you need someone to support your change efforts, consider a coach, a paid accountability program, or proposing a buddy to hold you accountable with a hefty consequence.

Myth 3: "Go cold turkey" or "All or nothing" mindsets work for most dudes

I've seen it hundreds of times...friends or colleagues try to make a change and shoot for the moon from the start. They decide to start a five-day-a-week exercise regime or completely overhaul their entire diet on a whim. Failure is almost always the result.

In all honesty, there are some people who succeed by going cold turkey or diving into a full-blown habit change instead of easing into it. But the vast majority don't.

Have I ever succeeded with the "Go cold turkey" or "All or nothing" mindsets? Actually I have, on several occasions. In each case there were specific circumstances that led to success:

1. **Previous failures:** Many habit changes that appear to happen instantly are deceiving.

"Appear" is the key word. Before "instantly" succeeding at meditating and exercising weekly, I failed dozens of times. Friends, colleagues, and other people just didn't see these failures. The habits just appeared to start "instantly" around occasions when people commonly change habits: new year's and Lent.

2. **Easy changes:** Making my bed every day and writing six days a week were incredibly simple habits to start. There was no trial and error of brief accomplishment and then failure. I succeeded with the habits on the first go and have had no interruption since I began them in 2017. With that said, they were both incredibly easy habits to integrate into my life. You are likely to have the same outcome when changing easy habits.

What about quitting cold turkey? When I quit smoking ten years ago, it also "appeared" to happen instantly. I didn't slowly reduce my cigarette count from week to week. So it probably seemed to many people that I just stopped suddenly. But like the habits mentioned above, there were many failed attempts before then. For this reason, I suggest you take **baby steps** (discussed in Chapter 4) and slowly integrate challenging habits into your life. You'll have a higher success rate.

Myth 4: Only change one habit at a time

"Changing one habit at a time" is not really a mainstream belief. Instead it's a style of habit change recommended in Leo Babauta's *The Power of Less*. While the book is excellent, changing multiple habits at a time isn't too hard. You just need to choose your habits wisely. During my year of changing eight habits, I often changed multiple habits during the same period. Does that mean you can change **any** two habits simultaneously?

Not exactly. Instead change habits that complement each other, or which at least don't clash.

Habit	Writing	Alcohol	Coffee
Week 1 (Aug 27)	Fri: Travel AM Sat: Travel AM	Thurs: 2 beers Sat: 1 beer	Fri: 1 coffee
Week 2 (Sept 3)	Fri: Travel AM Sat: Travel AM	Weds: 3 beers Sun: Champagne	Fri: 1 coffee
Week 3 (Sept 10)	Fri: Travel AM Sat: vacation	Tues: 3 beers Sun: 3 glass wine, 2 beers	Thurs: 1 coffee
Week 4 (Sept 17)	Fri: Travel AM Sun: Travel AM	Sat: 2 beers. 2 wine	0 coffee
Week 5 (Sept 24)	Write Fri & Sat	Weds: many beers	Thurs: 1 coffee
Week 6 (Oct 2)	Fr: Travel AM Sat: Travel AM	Fri: 2 big beers & glass of wine	Sat: 1 coffee
Week 7 (Oc 9)	Fri: Enlight AM Sat: Enlight AM	Sat: wasted	Thurs: 1 coffee
Week 8 (Oct 16)	Fri & Sat	Thurs - 3 glasses	Weds: 1 coffee

During an eight-week period from Aug-Oct 2017, I changed the above three habits: reduce my coffee and alcohol intake, and write six days a week[2]. Coffee and alcohol reduction complemented each other nicely, as I was aiming to reduce both beverages to just one day a week. The writing didn't really complement, but it also didn't clash with the other two. Clashing is really what you want to avoid.

For example, in the summer of 2017 I simultaneously attempted two habit changes—to cut back on coffee and wake up an hour early. This experiment failed miserably. And you can imagine why. The habits clash on a fundamental level, as I, like many dudes, used coffee as a crutch to wake up.

So changing multiple habits simultaneously is doable, just make sure the new habits don't clash.

---

[2] You may have noticed I only list two days of writing per week in the above image (typically Friday and Saturday), but claim I have a writing habit of six days a week. What gives? My day job is a copywriter at a marketing agency Monday-Thursday. As I'm writing there every day, I just need to make up the other two days later in the week. You with me?

Chapter 3

The crucial link between goals and habits

Goals and habits aren't so different. In fact, I'm guessing the reason you're interested in habit change is tied directly to a goal. Want to lose weight, quit smoking, or save $10,000 this year? The result is the goal, the habits are the path to success.

In this chapter, you'll learn how habits relate to goals and the crucial role they play in your success.

3 lessons in habit change—How I saved up to travel the world making $14 an hour

Like many dudes in their 20s, I once had a dream to travel the world for months on end. But back when I was 26, I had a bit of a problem. I was broke, making only $14 an hour. How on earth would I save up the money to realize my dream?

I documented the experience and strategies I used in my book *Backpack Abroad Now!* While it took me an entire year to accomplish my goal, during that year I learned three valuable lessons about habit change.

Lesson 1: Start with a clear goal

World travel had been a goal of mine since my late teens. But the dream didn't actually materialize until I developed a clear picture of what I wanted. By the time I was 26, I knew it was now or never. I had to take action. So I started thinking more about how I could travel for an extended period and what the trip would look like.

Southeast Asia stuck out to me as an ideal destination because it was cheap and I could experience many cultures, since multiple countries were clustered together. So that would be my goal: I would travel in and around Southeast Asia for a minimum of five months.

Let me repeat that...I would travel in and around Southeast Asia for a minimum of five months.

Do you see the clarity of that goal? I name where: Southeast Asia. I name how long: minimum of five months.

While having this goal helped me succeed, reflecting on it eight years later I realize I could have been much clearer. In other words, I could have done a better job. For example, I could have said, "By September 5, 2010, I will save up $6,000 and travel to Vietnam, Thailand, Australia, China, the Philippines, Indonesia, and Cambodia for six months."

That is way better. "Where" is defined much more clearly, a deadline is set, and an exact amount of savings is named.

Why is a clear goal important?

As the old cliché goes, you need to know where you're going to get there. A clear goal provides a target. Without one, you don't know where the end destination is, whether you succeeded or failed, or the actions necessary to progress. And because you don't know what you want, the likely result is inaction—and your habit or goal remains only wishful thinking.

How can you create a clear goal for yourself? Ask yourself if it passes the following four tests. Is your goal...

1. **Measurable**: Will you know if you succeeded or failed? As mentioned earlier, a deadline can help. If I didn't travel abroad by September 5, 2010, I would know I had failed.

2. **Concrete**: Is your goal tangible? Will you know when you achieved it? Concrete means your goal exists in the real world. Vietnam, Thailand, and all the other countries I listed are real, physical places. Once I arrived, there would be no doubt in my mind that I had achieved my goal.

3. **Specific**: Similar to concrete, but slightly different, a specific goal is exact. It's important that your goal is both specific and concrete, because sometimes a concrete goal is not very specific. For example, "travel abroad" is actually somewhat concrete. You'll have no doubt in your mind you've crossed the border of the US (or wherever you may live). But it's not exact. Where exactly do you want to travel abroad? China, Australia, and Thailand are very specific. And you could actually be even more specific: naming exact locations in each country you wish to visit. For example, The Great Wall of China, the Grand Palace in Bangkok, or the Whitsunday Islands in Australia.

4. **Within your control:** Are there steps you can take to achieve your goal? Earning $6,000 is possible, as I could control how much money I saved. No, it would not be easy, but I could reduce my cost of living, or work more hours to make more money.

If your goal is all the above, then it is clear enough to accomplish. Before moving on, let's look at one more example...let's say your goal is to <u>eat healthier</u>, which is a perfect example of an unclear goal.

Is it measurable? Definitely not. There's no deadline or criteria for eating healthier that tells you whether you've succeeded or failed.

Concrete? Nope again. "Eating healthier" is abstract; you don't know what it means in real-world terms.

Specific? If it's not concrete, it's probably not specific. So define exactly what it means to "eat healthier." Maybe it means eating until you're 80% full, or chowing down on four cups of veggies a day.

Within your control? Eating healthier is not in your control because you don't lay out the steps you need to get there. You don't know "how" to eat healthier because it isn't defined.

For me personally, I once said I was going to give up alcohol and carbs for five months. But as you may know, carbs are in everything (fruits and veggies are actually considered carbs). So how could I be more specific and concrete? I named the exact type of carb and changed my goal to "give up alcohol and all bread products for five months." Now, I had a concrete, specific goal that was measurable (I would easily know whether I had achieved it in five months) and within my control (the steps to success were to avoid all alcohol and bread products).

So what will your habit change look like? The above four qualities define the **end result** and the **steps to get there**. They provide you with a vision, a target to focus on, so you can accomplish anything you want.

Now let's return to the travel story. With a clear goal, I had to next figure out how I was going to get to Southeast Asia for at least five months. So I did something many Americans would consider unthinkable. I moved into a dining room...yes, the place families gather to eat.

Though it was slightly embarrassing, I somehow had two different girlfriends over that period, and they oddly enough accepted the fact I lived in a dining room...but I digress. Thankfully the dining room I moved into was empty, as the house was occupied by a bunch of dudes (who are also my close friends).

Of course, there's only one reason most people would move into a dining room. And that's to reduce costs. By making this somewhat absurd move, I effectively lowered my rent from $475 a month to $200. But that's not all I did. There is a key nugget of habit-changing wisdom here.

Lesson 2: Remind yourself daily of your habit goal

The uncomfortable conditions of the dining room were a perfect reminder of my travel goal. I had no door. Instead my room consisted of three walls and plenty of noise from the adjacent entertainment room. These living conditions were a daily reminder of the hidden habit I was changing, one I may not have always been consciously aware of: to spend less money.

Every day when I walked into my door-less room, every night as I blocked out noise from the living room with earplugs, every second I sat on my bed and saw the tile floors or heard the clank of dishes in the kitchen, I was reminded that I needed to save money. I knew if I were to get to the beaches, temples and parties of Asia, I had to get through the dining room. And to me, this space was the exact opposite of what I imagined Asia would be like. It was a trap. A cage. But in Asia...I would have freedom. I could travel where I wanted, experience new things each day, and live like a king on $1,000 a month.

The dining room served as a constant reminder of what I lacked. And I knew if I didn't change my habit and regularly save money, I'd be stuck in a room with no doors for god knows how long. So how can you apply this lesson?

I'm not saying go to the extreme and live in a dining room for a year so you can start saving. Instead, just give yourself some kind of reminder about your habit. Maybe that's simply a giant sign on your living room door that says, "Exercise, dude." Maybe it's a smartphone reminder on your phone every day that tells you to stop smoking. Whatever you choose, a reminder will make it easier to change. And, if that reminder is somewhat painful, like my dining room move, then your odds of success increase exponentially.

Me, finally out of the dining room and on The Great Wall of China in 2011.

While a reminder can provide the focus to change, there's another, even more important lesson here.

Lesson 3: Prioritize your goals and habits

In *An Ordinary Dude's Guide to Meditation*, I touch on prioritization near the end of the book. However, prioritization is so important it deserves a longer discussion. The process of prioritization I'm about to explain has changed my life in countless ways. You wouldn't be reading this book (as it wouldn't exist) if it weren't for the process I'm about to teach you. To change a difficult habit, you must prioritize it. But what does that mean?

When I moved into the dining room, I gave more importance to my goal of traveling abroad than anything else. I dedicated my life to the new habits of saving money and planning an extended trip overseas, which were two habits I practiced weekly.

How to prioritize effectively

I used to think I knew how to prioritize. But I didn't really "get it" until I read Brian Tracy's book *Eat That Frog!* In this book, Tracy explains the ABC prioritization method. The system is simple enough, and I use it every week as I plan my schedule. Here's how it works.

At the beginning of each week (typically Sundays for me), I write down everything I want to accomplish in the next seven days.

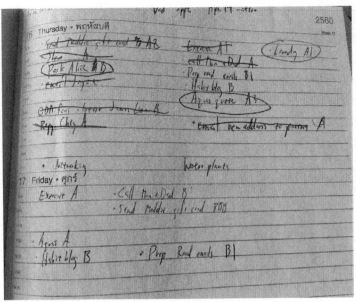

A sample of this method in action, from a page of my weekly planner in 2017. Please excuse the messy handwriting.

Each task is labeled with an A, B, or C. These letters denote the importance of the task.

- A is a top-priority task
- B is important, but not the end of the world if you don't complete it
- C is not that big of a deal if you don't finish it

The numbers 1, 2 and 3 next to each letter, note the importance and order of which you should accomplish the task. "A" is the most important and should be accomplished first. A1 is second most important and should be completed next, and so on.

You'll notice, however, there are no C tasks in my planner. I typically don't bother with them, but Tracy recommends them nevertheless.

It's up to you to decide what tasks are most important (Hint: your new habit should be an A task). Once you determine this, you'll then schedule your A tasks into your planner or calendar first, and then add B and C tasks when there is time available. Essentially, you plan your whole week around your A tasks.

Be careful of how many A tasks you schedule

Each of us has only so much time in a day, week, month, or year. You can only accomplish so much. As such, I highly recommend minding how many A tasks you take on.

For example, let's say you want to start the following four habits in the next three months:

- Blogging twice a week
- Reading a book a month
- Exercising three times a week
- Taking weekly tango classes

This is a recipe for failure. Almost any ordinary dude, myself included, would not be able to change all these habits in a three-month period. There is too much change in too small a window. So the principle to keep in mind here is:

The more A tasks you have to accomplish, the less likely you'll complete them.

So you need choose wisely. Integrating these four A tasks into your week would be borderline impossible because most of us don't have the time. You likely have a job, maybe a family, and probably enjoy somewhat of a life hanging out with your buddies. If you tried to incorporate all these habits so quickly, you'd have to de-prioritize something else. Which brings us to another key principle...

When you put something in, you must take something out.

You do not have an infinite amount of time and energy. No one does. This means it's not possible to continually add tasks to your schedule without it becoming overloaded and eventually unmanageable. With this idea in mind, think about what you'll remove from your schedule to accommodate your new habit.

If you want to exercise three times a week for an hour each session, where will you get those three hours? What will you give up? Maybe it's an hour of TV each night. Maybe it's some beer drinkin' with your buds.

Whatever it is, think about it beforehand. This will prevent you from becoming blindsided by your lack of time later on and wondering why you're too busy. If you decide what to take out before you start, lack of time will not be a reason for habit failure.

If you have too many A tasks, how do you choose?

Let's say you've found yourself in a pickle. You have 20 A tasks to complete this week and aren't sure which ones to prioritize. Certainly, some of your A tasks are non-negotiable—you have to complete them. For example, a doctor's appointment could be one, as could filing your taxes. Have kids? Well, taking care of those little buggers will certainly be an A task. But what happens when you have a conflict of A tasks that aren't obligatory, but you want to complete? What then?

I run into this very same problem at least once a month. And I resolve it by asking one simple question...

"Which task will make a bigger difference in my life?"

Hopefully, it's your new habit. And in all honesty, if it's not, you may want to hold off on it until a later date. Regardless, this simple question can keep your mind focused on the important things when hundreds of different tasks, people, and distractions are calling for your attention.

Once you've decided which tasks and habits to focus on, how can you ensure success? It all starts with making a plan.

Schedule your habits

When starting a new habit, I've found scheduling it in your planner (as shown in the image earlier) is one of the most effective ways to ensure it gets done. After your habit has become second nature and you're completing it on autopilot, it's not always necessary to schedule it as an A, B, or C task.

Today, I no longer schedule exercise as an A task, although I do write it down unlettered in my planner, just so I'm thinking about what days to exercise every week. The truth is, to accomplish your habit change, you just need to deliberately plan to do it. The simplest way to do that is, **write it down**.

Whether you write it down on your calendar, planner, or to-do list makes no difference. Just get it down in a place that you are regularly checking. It sounds ridiculous and too simple, but it's crazy how much of a difference writing something down has on your success rate. I've talked with other people about this and seen the magic of it first-hand in my own life. Whenever I write something down, 95% of the time I complete the task.

Though writing your habit down is great, there's something else you can do to increase your chances of success. Write down **exactly when and where** you'll perform your new habit. Is it going to be 8:35am in your bedroom? Right before lunch at 11am, are you going to go use the pool at your apartment for a swim? See how clear these examples are.

So, why does being clear on the details matter? In Chip and Dan Heath's excellent book *Switch*, they call this tactic an "action trigger." The authors note how action triggers preload a decision so you don't have to think about it. Us dudes are visual creatures, and an action trigger provides a visual of where and when you'll perform an activity. It is much more difficult to forget something when you visualize it.

Again, be clear on when and where you'll complete your habit. Then write it down in your calendar and move forward with it as scheduled.

The one-two punch: Writing a task down, followed by an action trigger uppercut

When it comes to habit change, combining action triggers with writing a task down is a force to be reckoned with. Let me give you an example from summer of 2017, during an exceptionally busy period of my life where I was taking weekly salsa classes, trying to incorporate three new habits into my routine, planning a trip to Malaysia, and doing the day job, among other tasks.

At dinner one night, my girlfriend asked if I was free on Wednesday night. I paused briefly and said, "Yep, what do you want to do?"

She was surprised, and asked, "How do you know you're free off the top of your head?"

I won't lie, I don't have the sharpest memory, which is why she was somewhat surprised about my quick answer. But I now know my quick response was because my calendar was ingrained in my head. Why is this?

As mentioned earlier, every Sunday I take an hour to plan my week, writing down every single important task, appointment, dinner date, party, etc. Typically, I schedule evening activities in my calendar to happen immediately after work. In this case, the action trigger isn't tied to a specific time of day, but rather an event: leaving the office. When I step out of the office elevator and walk towards the street, that's the action trigger for me to head to the afterwork event. By writing this meeting down in my planner and thinking about the action trigger, in this case leaving work, I am ingraining that task in my head.

The tactic of writing down exact times, events, and locations to complete something is so effective, that you could ask me what I have going on each evening on any given week, and I could answer you in seconds off the top of my head. This is because when you write down what you're doing at a specific time, you automatically create an action trigger that sticks in your brain.

Final thoughts on the link between goals and habit change

Everything you've read in this chapter up to this point—clear goals, reminders, prioritization, and action triggers—coincides with the major role goals play in habit change: they give you a target to shoot for.

In the first chapter, I mentioned some superdudes (Walt Disney, Stephen King, and Thomas Edison) who accomplished remarkable things. No doubt, these visionaries had clear goals that helped them succeed. But were goals the sole reason for their achievements?

One thing these superdudes have in common is passion. Passion is fuel for big goal accomplishment. When you love what you're doing, when you love the process, you can push past repeated failures. But can passion help with habits?

Well, as mentioned in the introduction, the habit change process is quite boring. While Disney loved animating Mickey Mouse, most dudes trying to lose weight aren't passionate about eating less pizza. In other words, passion doesn't really help with habits. So if passion can't motivate your habit change, what can? How can you increase your odds of success?

There are many books out there that talk about finding your purpose, your *why*. And while some of these books may seem to lack substance, identifying your *why* is extremely important to achieving any goal or daunting habit change.

What is a *why*?

It's your crystal clear reward: when you achieve your goal, what exactly do you win? I touched on this briefly in Lesson 1 of this chapter. For my backpacking trip, my *why* was freedom, travel, and new experiences. When I quit bread products and alcohol for five months, my *why* was to heal my feet and move on with my life.

Are you starting to see the importance of knowing your *why*?

When you have a bad day, when you fail, when you feel defeated...on days you question what the purpose of it all is...when you feel like giving up on your dreams or habit...your *why* is what keeps you going. It motivates you to pick your head up, dust yourself off, and move forward.

While your goal is the target, your *why* is the reward for winning. It's the motivating force that keeps you going.

In the first chapter, I mentioned how "The small picture and the easy way out" is a major habit stumbling block. Your *why*, however, is your remedy. So I'd like to share with you a tactic I use when life punches me in the face. When you suffer a major setback, I want you to take a minute, sit yourself down, and say the following two words—big picture.

Once you do that, remember your crystal clear goal. Visualize your reward and remind yourself there is something bigger you're chasing.

Instead of thinking about the pizza you can't eat, think about how awesome you'll feel when you're 20 pounds lighter. Think about the chicks or studs who will want to get in your pants when you're leaner and more fit.

Fuck the process. Think about the reward.

I can't tell you how many times the **big picture tactic** has kept me moving forward on a bad day. Simply say those two words, remind yourself of your long-term goal, and then imagine your reward.

All challenges are temporary setbacks

In 2017, I read *The Everything Store* by Brad Stone, which is the true story of how Jeff Bezos built the online behemoth Amazon. There was one simple lesson I took from the book that made reading it worthwhile.

As you probably know, Amazon is one of the biggest companies in the world. But it wasn't always that way. The company began like many business success stories: starting in a garage, moving office to a dumpy warehouse, and slowly improving year after year.

What many people may not know, however, is that Amazon wasn't profitable for nearly a decade. In fact, some of Amazon's most popular services have cost the company dearly. For example, a Forrester analyst once estimated that Amazon was losing $1 billion a year on Prime-related shipping expenses. Yet Bezos believed in the service. He knew, and still knows that Prime is a mechanism for fostering customer loyalty, and is unwilling to sacrifice long-term profits for short-term gains.

Prime is a brilliant example of Bezos' commitment to a long-term vision. While Amazon started as an online bookstore, he always imagined it as much more—a store where you could buy everything online cheaply and have it shipped to you fast. Bezos knew that if he could increase customer loyalty by offering cheap products customers loved, he could eventually create an empire. So what's the lesson in all this?

On a large enough timeline, anything is possible.

When you have a grand vision, when you look at the big picture, all obstacles can be viewed as temporary setbacks. Reading *The Everything Store*, it becomes apparent that seeing all setbacks as temporary is a guiding philosophy at Amazon. When Prime was losing money for years, it was just a temporary setback. When the Fire phone bombed and lost a reported 170 million dollars, it was again a temporary setback. In the short term, both these obstacles could have seemed like a catastrophe. But when viewed from a long-term perspective, they could be seen as a minor bump on the long highway to achieving great things. How can this apply to you?

When you cheat on your diet, miss a day of exercise, succumb to the allure of a cigarette, or when things don't go as planned, keep your eye on the long-term vision. Know that the bad days, frustrations, and even big failures are just temporary setbacks: bumps in the road on the path to your goal. But, that's only true if you pick yourself up and keep moving forward. So don't give up. Combine your big picture vision with substance—the clear goals, reminders, prioritization, and action triggers—and you now have stepping stones to achieving anything you want.

Of course, there's still more to it. In the next chapter, we're going to get more into the meat of habit change, and learn specific tactics you can use to win your habit.

Chapter 4

Tactics for habit change domination

In previous chapters, we've touched on several tactics to alter your habits. Extreme accountability, action triggers, prioritization, and altering your environment, among others. In this chapter, we're going to dive deeper into a series of other tactics that can complement what you've already learned, starting with a time-tested strategy that's worked wonders for me.

When is the easiest time to get your habit on?

Among many habit authors and experts, the morning is glorified as an optimal time for habit building. And for good reason. At this time, there are no distractions. But, of course, you may not be a morning dude (me neither), so it's incredibly tempting to push your habit off to the evening. What happens then?

Well, there's a chance an unexpected activity—like drinks with friends, an important meeting, or sleepiness or exhaustion—bumps your habit aside. In *An Ordinary Dude's Guide to Meditation*, I describe how these obstacles prevented my everyday meditation habit from sticking. How did I overcome them? A simple switch to meditating in the morning cleared up the problem immediately. And, finally, my every day meditation habit stuck.

Starting a habit in the morning can do the same for you. At this time, the call of the bar, your buddies, or your bed will less likely tempt you away from your habit. You have full control over your mornings.

With that said, another way to ensure success is to group habits together. For example, if you already have the habit of meditating, eating breakfast and then brushing your teeth, add another habit into this sequence. This process is often referred to as **habit stacking**, and there are entire books written about the technique. The philosophy behind habit stacking is that your current habits form an efficient network of neurons that are hard-wired into your brain. So when you add a new habit into this network, it sticks much more easily. Let's use an analogy to illustrate the concept...

Imagine you're trying to open up a t-shirt store. If you open a shop in a mall where there are plenty of profitable businesses established, you're more likely to feed off the other stores' success. The mall is the network. You're just adding your shop to an already proven system. On the other hand, if you open shop in the middle of nowhere with no businesses around, how will you attract customers? Well, you're going to have to start from scratch because you don't have a network. This will take more time and effort as you figure it out yourself. The same goes with habit.

I've successfully used habit stacking as I integrated two new routines into my schedule: making my bed and exercising. My sequence goes like this—meditate > make bed > exercise > eat breakfast > floss.

The meditation, breakfast, and floss habits were already well-ingrained. So I just slotted in two new ones, which made it easier for me to start and maintain my bed-making and exercise habits.

Experiment, experiment, experiment

As mentioned earlier, experimenting is key to habit change. A few weeks after starting your habit, take time to reflect, analyze what is and isn't working, and then make adjustments. If you failed, don't beat yourself up. Instead look at the process as trial and error. Reflect on why you failed and then test an alternative tactic next week. I reflect on successes and failures every Sunday as I plan the upcoming week. If a new habit change failed, I ask myself, "What was the reason?"

By examining your own missteps and successes, you can learn the most effective tactics and improve your odds of achieving lasting habit change.

Here's a similar process you can follow:

1. Choose a time and day to reflect on your habits
2. During this time, ask yourself, "What caused the failure?"
3. Hypothesize an alternative tactic to create success
4. Try this new tactic next week

Repeat this process each week as you search for a pattern that sticks.

By experimenting in this way, you're basically becoming a scientist for your life. And as a scientist, there's a key piece of information you'll need to measure success: data. Where do you get data? I recommend tracking your habits on a spreadsheet.

Habit	Writing	Alcohol	Coffee	NOTES
Week 1 (Aug 27)	Fri: Travel AM Sat: Travel AM	Thurs: 2 beers Sat: 1 beer	Fri: 1 coffee	
Week 2 (Sept 3)	Fri: Travel AM Sat: Travel AM	Weds: 3 beers Sun: Champagne	Fri: 1 coffee	
Week 3 (Sept 10)	Fri: Travel AM Sat: vacation	Tues: 3 beers Sun: 3 glass wine, 2 beers	Thurs: 1 coffee	Felt depressed in the evening on the day I had coffee
Week 4 (Sept 17)	Fri: Travel AM Sun: Travel AM	Sat: 2 beers. 2 wine	0 coffee	
Week 5 (Sept 24)	Write Fri & Sat	Weds: many beers	Thurs: 1 coffee	
Week 6 (Oct 2)	Fr: Travel AM Sat: Travel AM	Fri: 2 big beers & glass of wine	Sat: 1 coffee	
Week 7 (Oc 9)	Fri: Enlight AM Sat: Enlight AM	Sat: wasted	Thurs: 1 coffee	
Week 8 (Oct 16)	Fri & Sat	Thurs - 3 glasses	Weds: 1 coffee	

You may remember a version of the above sheet from Chapter 2. I created it in October 2017 as I successfully attempted to change three habits at once. Here's an explanation of the sheet's content, starting with the two colors[3] I used to document my successes and failures:

- Red - fail. I didn't achieve my goal.
- Green - success! Booyah!

Simple enough, right? As you can see, I noted the number of drinks I downed and the type of content I wrote. In this expanded image you'll also see a note taking column. While I only made notes once, you can use this column to see if there's a correlation between your feelings and a new habit. For example,

I thought coffee may have had something to do with a depressed mood I had one evening. But the sour feeling with coffee was a one-off occurrence, so there didn't seem to be a direct correlation. How can you use this method yourself?

Well, it doesn't have to be as complicated as the spreadsheet above. You can also track a single habit, like I did below.

Back exercises: May 21 - July 8		
3 Times per week.		
Habit	**Back exercise**	
Week 1 (May 21)	3 times	
Week 2 (May 28)	3 times	
Week 3 (June 4)	3 times	
Week 4 (June 11	3 times	
Week 5 (June 18	3 times	
Week 6 (June 25	3 times	
Week 7 (July 2)	3 times	

Above is a temporary habit I tracked from May to July 2018. My goal was to strengthen my back by exercising the muscles in it three times each week.

The simplicity of this data is obvious. Every Sunday I wrote down in my planner which days I'd exercise my back, and then the following Sunday I'd note in the spreadsheet how many times I followed through. As you can see, I had a 100% success rate.

How can a spreadsheet help you? Besides serving as a place to track data, the sheet helped me stay focused during a very busy time in my life. Focus is the secret sauce of spreadsheet tracking. This method uses two tactics from the previous chapter that help keep your eye on the prize. Firstly, the spreadsheet acts as a **reminder** to complete your habit and, secondly, you **write it down**.

While tracking is extremely helpful, there's always a chance an unforeseen obstacle could derail the whole process. So how do you prepare for that?

Your hidden obstacle

Half the battle of winning the habit change game is understanding your core roadblock. If you're confused as to why you've continually failed at a specific habit, there's likely something you're unaware of that's keeping you from success.

- Why is it every time you try to quit smoking, you end up with a cigarette between your lips outside the bar?
- Why is it every time you try to maintain an exercise routine, you end up feeling too exhausted to hit the gym?
- Why is it every time you try to save money, you end up blowing your savings on a shopping spree?

There is a reason. The question is, what is it for you?

Know your kryptonite

Kryptonite is exactly what it sounds like. It's your one weakness. The one deal-breaker that sabotages your chances of habit success.

Not all habits are vulnerable to kryptonite. But the stubborn ones almost always are. Out of the eight habits I changed in 2017, and the handful of others I've cemented in years past, the three most challenging habits were susceptible to kryptonite. These habits were starting a weekly exercise routine, practicing meditation every day, and reducing my coffee consumption to one cup a week. That said, I wasn't aware of habit kryptonite until 2017—when I finally conquered a habit I had wrestled with for over half a decade...

A regular exercise routine always eluded me. No matter how many attempts I made, the habit wouldn't last more than four months or so. But in December 2016, I was determined to end the series of losses. My goal was to exercise two to four times per week for the entire next year. I succeeded. And halfway through 2017, after many near failures in the preceding six months, I reflected on the instances I almost broke my habit. A hidden obstacle quickly emerged.

Sickness. Likely due to the chaos of the first half of 2017 and the dreaded Bangkok hot season, I was sick three times during that period. Nearly every time I was on the edge of quitting my habit. But I forced myself to continue. Once I recognized this pattern, I reflected on all the times my habit routine collapsed in the past half decade. The same pattern was always there. Every time I quit, I was sick.

The discovery of this pattern was a revelation to me. Now that I was aware of it, I could find a way to sidestep the obstacle. So I came up with a plan. Every time I got sick, I would alter my exercise routine. Instead of continuing the routine as normal, I'd reduce the time and effort I put into exercise. For example, now when I get sick, I do the absolute minimum amount of exercise. I exercise no more than two times a week, and I reduce my swimming time from 30 minutes to 10-15 minutes. Other times I won't swim at all. I simply do some jumping jacks, push ups, and/or stretches.

The amazing thing is, maintaining the habit (even in a mild form) helps keep it in motion. When I got sick in 2016 and years prior, I'd stop exercising altogether. And by the time I got better, I had forgotten all about my routine. Today I don't forget. I keep the habit wheels in motion, even while I'm sick, and the pattern carries on easily in full form once I've recovered.

For meditation, my kryptonite was "unexpected activities in the evening." To this day, my favorite time to meditate is between 6pm and 7pm after work. I love the feeling. It's a great way to unwind...kind of like a shower. It washes away the day's gunk, emotional baggage, and annoyances.

When I was meditating between 6pm and 7pm every day, I had no problem maintaining my habit five days a week. The problem was, five days a week wasn't good enough—I wanted to meditate every day. But I couldn't get over the hump. Something was holding me back. And when I started to reflect, the obstacle became clear.

There were a few times a week when unexpected activities would pop up in my schedule. Sometimes it would be drinks with friends. Sometimes it was a networking event. Either way, I'd leave directly after work to meet up, which meant I would miss my evening meditation. And if alcohol was ever involved (which it often was), there was no way I would make up my meditation later. So it finally occurred to me that this was my problem...unexpected events were my kryptonite. They were the one reason I wasn't meditating every day.

After I realized this, I started meditating first thing in the morning. And since then, it's been smooth sailing. I've been meditating every day for over four years now. The only time I skip it is if I need to get up extremely early in the morning (before 6am) or if I'm on vacation.

As for my coffee habit, the kryptonite was a different beast altogether, which brings up an interesting point.

Kryptonite comes in all shapes and sizes

To effectively set in a motion a tough habit, you need to understand the **root cause** of your failure. For me it was timing (for meditation) and sickness (for exercise). But coffee...coffee left me baffled. The habit was much more primal than meditating or exercising. What's more, this time I wasn't starting a habit. I was stopping one.

I didn't realize immediately what was causing me to struggle. Of course, caffeine is addictive. But I didn't think addiction had anything to do with why I couldn't reduce my coffee consumption[4]. All I knew was there was a strong urge to drink coffee. Thankfully, I came across *The Power of Habit* by Charles Duhigg at just the right time—mid-habit change.

In Duhigg's incredibly helpful book, he notes that to stop a bad habit, you often need to replace it with something else. As soon as I read this, I understood my coffee addiction kryptonite: I needed something else to drink. I immediately started swapping out the coffee for mango smoothies, aloe vera juice, chrysanthemum tea and other drinks, and it became much easier to make it through the mornings without coffee.

So there you have it: three different forms of kryptonite. But don't be deceived. Kryptonite is not limited to the examples above. Your friends, colleagues, and acquaintances can be kryptonite, too. As I'll discuss later in this book, the people you hang around with most can have a major influence on your habits.

With that said, the list of types of kryptonite can go on indefinitely. The trick is figuring out yours.

What is your kryptonite?

The first step to beating your kryptonite is knowing what it is. So let this question be your guide..."What is causing my habit to fail?"

Look for patterns. You may have to fail multiple times and experiment with different solutions before your kryptonite becomes clear. But once it does, then it's time to attack. Or, in other words, devise a plan.

The plan is generally incredibly simple. As mentioned, for meditation my kryptonite was events after work causing me to miss my practice. Once I identified the problematic pattern, the plan was easy: meditate at a time when no unexpected event can disrupt my activity—first thing in the morning.

When I reduced my alcohol consumption to two nights of boozing a week, I discovered it was susceptible to the same kryptonite as coffee. I needed something else to drink. Once I identified the replacement issue, I came up with a similar plan as I had for coffee and drank soda water instead of beer.

You're probably starting to notice a theme here. Kryptonite is beaten in two steps:

1. Identify the kryptonite
2. Plan how to maneuver around it

It's that simple. Ask yourself what's causing you to fail. Then once you identify the core obstacle, plan a strategy to sidestep the failure.

Baby Steps

You have a plan, you know your priorities, now what? The last step in this process is to take action. And that starts with taking one small step at a time. For example, if you want to start an exercise routine, there's no need to jump into six days a week from the get-go. That can be overwhelming. So start small and aim for one or two days a week, and then build on that. Once one or two days have been habitualized, bump that amount up to three, four, five, and then six.

With meditation, I always recommend people to start small as well. Jumping into a 20-minute session your first time will likely overwhelm you. It may leave such a bad taste in your mouth that you swear off meditation for good. So start with one minute, then two, five, ten, and so on. Build your confidence with those small wins, and then slowly work your way up to your ideal time.

Still struggling with your habit? When all else fails, find a model

If you've failed at your habit multiple times, there's no reason to feel continually frustrated and confused. I guarantee someone has changed the exact same habit you're trying to change now. He or she has been through your struggles and knows how to overcome them. So the way to master your habit is to find out what that person did and copy their behavior. This tactic is called modeling.

Modeling is perfect for habits ordinary dudes struggle with, like eating healthier, exercising regularly, or quitting smoking. For all these types of habit changes, there are books, support groups, and programs designed to help you. With that said, my goal in this book is to ensure you have everything you need to make your habit change—without relying on other resources. The above recommendation is a last-resort method. And before you even consider it, there's one model worth consulting that won't cost you a penny.

The dude staring back at you in the mirror

Yep, that's you, dude. You may just be the best model you could ever imagine. What do I mean? Well, look into your past. What habits have you successfully started in the previous five, 10, or 15 years? Surely there have been some.

One of the first habits I recall consciously forming was flossing my teeth. I was well aware I didn't floss, and my dentist continually reminded me of the fact. From this habit, I devised the tactic "perform your habit first thing in the morning," which I've modeled many times since.

Now it's your turn. Look to your past and ask yourself the following:

- What habits do you have now?

- What were some awesome habits you maintained for a year or longer, but then quit?
- How did you form these habits?
- Which tactics did you use to start and then maintain each habit?

Learning from your own successes can be hugely beneficial. So remember the patterns, behaviors, or actions you relied on to cement past habits, and then use those same tactics to start your new one. In other words, model your past behavior.

---

[3] You probably picked up on this, but if not, the darker shade in the spreadsheet is red and lighter shade is green.

[4] Through a lot of experimenting over the years, I've learned if I don't drink caffeine more than three days in a row, I won't suffer withdrawal if I stop suddenly. For at least a year prior to reducing my coffee consumption to one cup a week, I never drank caffeine more than three days in a row.

Chapter 5

Break old habits

When it comes to breaking habits, there are two schools of thought. The first involves exercising the willpower muscles (covered in Chapter 2), and the second is replacement (mentioned last Chapter).

For me, I've had experience with both willpower and replacement. And in this chapter, you'll learn how you can use both methods to break bad habits. Let's start off with the tactic more dudes are likely familiar with.

Letting temptation pass

If you've attempted to quit smoking, junk food, or binge-drinking, you've certainly been tempted to reach for that cigarette, chocolate, or bottle of whisky, and fought the urge as hard as you could. Sometimes you win, sometimes you lose.

Your success rate likely depends on two things:

1. How badly you want the new habit

2. Your amount of experience resisting temptation

Let's talk about number one first. If you badly want to break a habit, you likely have a long-term goal your new habit fulfills. As mentioned in Chapter 1 (The small picture and the easy way out) and the end of Chapter 3 (temporary setbacks), focusing on the long-term goal helps you resist the bad habit. And when combining this focus with other habit-changing strategies—like making a plan, baby steps, and knowing your kryptonite—your odds of success increase exponentially.

As for number two, experience resisting temptation, it counts for something. And there just so happens to be a perfect time of year to practice strengthening your willpower muscles.

The season for temptation resistance training

Many a dude says, "Practice makes perfect." And for this reason, I highly recommend participating in Lent, which I've been practicing for as long as I can remember. But wait a second, don't you have to be Christian to practice Lent?

There's no rule book. I haven't subscribed to any religion for over a decade, and I still practice Lent every year. Even my girlfriend (who is a Buddhist) has given up or tested out a new habit during the 40-day observation period.

Practicing Lent since I was a little dude has undoubtedly given me an advantage in altering my habits. Along the way, I've given up candy, alcohol, caffeine, sex, watching NBA basketball, and more—with about a 90% success rate. The point is, no matter your religious affiliation, or lack thereof, Lent can help you learn more about your habit kryptonite, exercise your willpower muscles, and build confidence in changing your habits.

As with gaining experience in anything, you'll get a better understanding of yourself and your weaknesses, and start to learn effective strategies for tackling habits. For example, when I locked in my meditation habit during a 40-day period after Lent, I learned the importance of action triggers and devising a strategy.

Wait, 40-day period after Lent? Yes, you heard that correctly. I started my routine meditation practice during a 40-day period following Lent. This means if you'd rather not participate because you're not Christian, you can simply borrow the Lent concept and apply it to another period of days, weeks, or months during the year.

Lent or not, a period of days testing a new routine has benefits (and can be fun)

Remember in the introduction where I asked you to imagine being someone else for a day? A period of days experimenting with a new habit is the perfect time to try on another pair of shoes and test a different lifestyle.

How will you feel if you exercise five times a week for 60 days? What about if you quit soda for 30 days? Will you accomplish more if you wake an hour earlier for 40 days? Seeing and experiencing the results of your habit experiment can be quite fun. You may feel different, you may act differently, and you may even look different. And while it's true that testing out a new habit could be a bust, maybe...just maybe...it could change your life. But there's only one way to find out, and that's by giving it a try.

The time of year you test your new routine matters not, but be aware of approaching events and holidays that could derail your efforts. For example, you may have heard of the concept cheat days; I actually have a cheat month. December. I never tweak habits around Christmas season as I typically overindulge in everything.

As for the number of days you practice, I'd recommend somewhere between 30 and 60. Less than 30 days and the dramatic mood and psychological differences of habit change may not yet occur. And more than 60 days, unless you're a hundred percent sure you want to change your habit (and not just test-drive it), is probably too long. A 60-day period provides you more than enough time to see whether you want to continue it permanently or go back to the way things were.

Whether your goal is to test or instill a new habit, dedicating a time of year to habit change will reveal new insights about yourself. For example, I wasn't aware of the compounding effect Thailand's heat had on my alcohol and caffeine habits until I gave them up during two separate Lent periods in Bangkok.

By avoiding these stimulants for long periods, I suddenly became aware of how my body performed without them: I was no longer getting dehydrated all the time. So I devised a theory that heat wasn't the only cause of my habitual dehydration—coffee and alcohol were playing a significant role. I later tested this theory on an extended Christmas holiday in the US, returning to my typical alcohol and caffeine consumption habits. What do you know? I wasn't getting dehydrated like I was in Bangkok, which has led me to believe that I need to watch how much alcohol and caffeine I drink in Thailand...at least if I don't want to be chronically dehydrated.

The point of this story is that a 30-, 40-, 50-, or whatever-day period of habit change, will give you key insights into how different foods, drinks, or new habits impact your life. It's an experiment. And the results, as you can see, can be quite revealing.

This isn't the only reason I recommend a Lent like period in your life. You can also use an extended period of habit change to spark a new routine, much like how people use the new year to start or stop a new behavior. The 40-day period gives you a definitive starting point to test-drive a habit. And sometimes the habit sticks. Like I mentioned earlier, I restarted my daily meditation practice during a 40-day period immediately after Lent in 2014 and it's still going strong to this day.

When it comes to breaking habits, the extended recess also gets you used to the feeling of resisting urges and letting them pass.

Resisting temptation

You can feel it. The urge creeps up on you. Your legs begin to shake as you try to fight the temptation, but your mind is consumed with cigarettes or junk food. How can you resist? If you could just have one smoke, or one bite of cake, then it would all be fine.

The urge builds like a wave, begging, screaming for you to indulge...you tell yourself, "No, this is not what I want." Giving in will feel good now, but only hurt later. I want a smoke-free life. I want a healthier diet. I want to move on with my life...and then, suddenly, it breaks. The urge begins to wane.

When resisting temptation, realize the urge builds till it reaches a crescendo, breaks, and then begins to subside. To get to the breaking point, generally you need to take your mind off the temptation. In other words, focus on something else.

You can think about the big picture or your reward. You can focus on your breath as if you were meditating. You can focus on the sounds of the wind rustling, or even turn on the TV to change your mindset. When resisting temptation, distraction is a solid option. Act as if you're trying to distract a crying two-year-old (but, in this case, you're the crying two-year-old). Focus your mind on something else, and the problem goes away.

If you don't react to the urge, it will pass. More urges will come, yes, but they'll weaken each time until they disappear altogether.

Is this method painful? Yes, even after personally following this method for years, it's still a challenge. When you're dealing with a deeply ingrained habit, it almost never gets easier. Which is why I'm thankful I discovered what I deem a better alternative option to breaking habits.

Replace your bad habit with something else

Let's more closely examine the replacement strategy. On the surface the tactic is easy enough: simply replace your bad habit with something else. Smokers (whether they're conscious of it or not) have been using this method for decades as they replace cigarettes with Nicorette or gum. With that said, this replacement tactic can be applied to any habit. You simply need to discover the driving force behind it. To give an example, let's revisit *The Power of Habit*. In his book, Charles Duhigg describes his bad habit of getting a cookie every day around 3pm. But what urge was the cookie satisfying? The urge to eat? Or was it something else?

After experimenting with different replacements for the cookie, Duhigg discovered the true cause of his habit had nothing to do with hunger, but instead to get a temporary distraction from work. He had an urge to take a break, and leaving his desk to buy a cookie satisfied just that need.

How to discover the urge driving your bad habit

The key is to experiment with different options. If you're a smoker, maybe your primary urge to smoke has nothing to do with nicotine. For example, my urge to smoke was much like Duhigg's urge for a cookie. While quitting, I discovered the driving force behind the habit was to get a temporary break and some fresh air. So when the urge to smoke arose, I started going for walks instead and the habit began to fade.

What I replaced alcohol with during my five-month hiatus

Do you remember the story in Chapter 1 where I gave up alcohol for five months? The most challenging part of that ordeal was going straight into the hornet's nest, a bar, and refusing to drink. Just how did I do this? While I didn't realize it at the time, looking back I can clearly see I replaced beer at the bar with an alternative—chewing tobacco.

I've been an on-and-off chewing tobacco enthusiast for years, but never so much as when I gave up alcohol for five months. Again, I had no idea I was replacing my urge to drink with another stimulant, but it was effective nevertheless. Once that wad of tobacco was placed under my lip, no longer did I crave beer. Granted, I was replacing one bad habit with another, so it wasn't the best alternative.

These days, however, I still use this tactic, but with typically healthier replacements. Instead of coffee, I drink tea or smoothies. Instead of alcohol, I reach for a soda water or juice. So for you, next time you're about to quit a habit, ask yourself, "What can I replace it with?"

You may find the answer to breaking your most frustrating habit.

Chapter 6

The power of influence: You become what you consume

You may have heard of the idea "you are the reflection of the five people you most hangout with." Like many people, I simply used to brush aside this phrase as something people said. But as I've gotten older, I see the truth in this statement more than ever. The people we hang out with have an incredible influence on us.

I once saw a friend of mine, a typically laid-back dude, suddenly transform into a critical, demanding jerk. What was the cause? Almost certainly his new, short-tempered girlfriend...he returned to normal after they broke up a few years later. A similar pattern played out with a former girlfriend of mine. She started a job with a rude boss, and before I knew it, she was acting rudely towards me, even using some of his phrases verbatim. Once she quit, those rude habits began to fade.

Hang around with your models

In Chapter 4, I mentioned how copying a model's behavior can be beneficial when changing a particularly stubborn habit. As the people you hang with have a tremendous influence on you, you should jump at the chance to regularly interact with your models.

In 2014, I did exactly this. I wanted to quit my job to become a full-time freelance writer. And while I didn't know any freelancers at the time, I was aware of an online community called the Freelance Writer's Den. There I could interact with and learn from experienced freelancers, some who made over six figures a year.

I joined the Den in June with the goal to quit my day job in September. After I signed up, I dived deep into the community's online resources, asked questions in the forum, and learned as much as I could about the behaviors of successful freelancers. By the time September rolled around, I had not only gained a small client base, but I also quit my job as planned. What's more, the following month I made the most money I had ever earned in Bangkok. My freelance writing brought in 35% more income in October than my day job had in September. I could never have done this without the influence and support of the online community.

With that said, the Freelance Writer's Den is not my only example of how an online community can influence habits and mindset. In July 2017, I joined the incredible Mastering Amazon Ads Facebook group and saw sales of *An Ordinary Dude's Guide to Meditation* explode from a few copies a month to regularly over a hundred—all within just six months of joining.

As dudes you regularly associate with have a tremendous influence on you, I highly recommend spending as much time as possible around positive influences. And if you can't physically hang with them, you can usually find them online.

Get in the habit of engaging with positive influences

Of course, hanging out with the right people doesn't give you a free pass to do nothing. You must also actively engage with them. If I'd joined the Freelance Writer's Den or Mastering Amazon Ads and participated sparingly, I would've gotten nowhere. At a minimum, you need to learn from the group and model their behavior. And if you engage regularly, you'll likely adopt new habits automatically as the influence of the group naturally rubs off on you. Of course, though, good people aren't the only thing to surround yourself with.

The influence of food, video, music, and more

When it comes to changing your behavior, people are just one piece of the puzzle. There's also a slew of other things that influence demeanor, that many dudes are either not aware of or simply gloss over.

Remember the old saying, "you are what you eat"? Well, I believe that statement to be true...the food and drinks you down can have a huge impact on your mood, health, productivity, and behavior. I become a regular drama queen when I guzzle too much booze or caffeine. I'll become irritable, overreact to little problems, and just generally feel unstable. In other words, I become a mess. As mentioned, too much caffeine and alcohol consumption for me personally bring on dehydration, which causes a boatload of other problems, like difficulty sleeping and flared-up psoriasis. It's not pleasant. But when I reduce the consumption of these stimulants, all those issues disappear naturally.

Outside of stimulants, you likely know how a heavy meal can cause lethargy, and how sweet drinks can just as quickly boost your energy levels as cause a sugar crash. The problem is, your body may become desensitized to the sensations of whatever you regularly consume. Why? Because you've grown accustomed to it. This is why experimenting and avoiding a specific food or stimulant for a period of days can reveal insights about how it affects your mood and psyche.

The influence of outside forces doesn't stop with food, stimulants, and people. The music you listen to, the videos you watch, the news you read—all of them influence your behavior. Let me share an example. Just a few years after the release of the movie *An Inconvenient Truth*, global warming news stories were still popular. Concerned about the future of the world, I read all of them. Unfortunately, none of them had good news...all the stories said we were screwed. And, well, it was depressing. That year, in 2008, tired of being frustrated by the global warming downer, I decided to give up news for Lent.

Within a few weeks after the purge, I couldn't believe how much clearer my head was, and how much more stable I felt. The point is, influences come in all shapes and sizes.

If you're in a grumpy mood regularly, if you're always broke, if you have some kind of health problem that won't go away, take stock of your consumption habits. Reflect and ask yourself, "What might I be consuming that could cause this negative effect?"

Become the experimenter and then test removing a habit or adding a new one, and see if it makes a difference.

Chapter 7

Do you believe you can change?

During my freshman-year of college, my philosophy professor, Dr. Hahn, once shared a story that sticks in my mind to this day...

He was at a bar and sat next to two dudes who looked like regulars. In walked a beautiful woman who took a seat at the opposite end of the room. One of the regulars looked to his buddy and said, "Wouldn't it be great to have a gorgeous girl like that?"

The other replied, "Yeah, too bad we'll never get one." The regulars nodded in agreement and then continued drinking their beers.

Dr. Hahn told our class, those guys will never date her or any beautiful woman because they don't believe they can. In fact, they won't even try because they believe she's out of their league. Even if she did approach one of them, which is doubtful, they'd surely screw it up as they feel unworthy of such a beauty.

The point is, belief plays a huge role in your ability to change habits or accomplish anything. If you don't believe you can change, you simply won't.

Me personally, I've never been much of a belief guy. I'm not a religious dude, nor do I believe in much of anything. But I know for everything I've accomplished—from traveling the world for 11 months, changing dozens of habits, to becoming a full-time writer and author—it all started with belief. I believed I could realize my goal. If I didn't believe, I would've never tried. Belief is fundamental to any change.

Fake it till you make it, affirmations, and belief myths

Just like there are habit myths, there are also belief myths. And perhaps the biggest misconception about belief is that believing is simple—all you have to do is *fake it till you make it*. Some dudes believe success will materialize if you act as though you've already succeeded. But it's not a given. Without belief, repeating affirmations or dressing the part become empty promises that can lead to self-delusion and denial.

While I have nothing against positive affirmations, the problem occurs when dudes don't believe the messages they tell themselves, or alter their behavior to align with the affirmation. For example, if you affirm you're going to drop 20 pounds, but still eat a box of Twinkies every other day, that beer belly ain't going away. If you repeatedly say, "I am a millionaire" for months on end but do nothing but sit on the couch all day watching *Survivor,* your chances of making that mill are slim to none. Why is this? Affirmations and *faking it till you make it* don't address the root problem. There needs to come a tipping point when faking it transforms into a legit, internal belief. Do that and you can truly achieve anything.

7 steps to ignite belief

Affirmations alone fall short because they lack a plan, strategy, and vision. And you may not have noticed, but this book provides a roadmap for the latter three. In other words, within these pages is a blueprint on how to create belief. The exact steps are scattered throughout, so here they are in order:

- **Step 1: Find your *why***
  It all starts here. Before you develop a strategy and vision, you need to know what you truly want. So ask yourself, "What would make me

most happy?" and then define exactly what your reward looks like. No matter if you're chasing a simple habit change or a million dollars, your *why* is your belief engine.

- **Step 2: Experiment, experiment, experiment**
  Most dudes attempting to change a habit already know their *why* (and if that's you, you can skip this step). But for those in search of a bigger goal, who don't know what they want in their career, relationships or life, then lifestyle experimentation can help. Think you want to be a pharmacist? Volunteer at a drugstore for a few months to see if you enjoy it. Want to find the gal or guy of your dreams? Jump on Tinder or another app and go on a dating rampage to discover the ideal characteristics of your perfect partner. Test, test, and test until you find what you're looking for.

- **Step 3: Formulate a clear, specific goal**
  You know your *why*. You know what you want. Now it's time to design the grand vision of your ambition. Define a measurable, concrete, and specific goal that's within your control.

- **Step 4: Remind yourself daily of your goal**

If you like affirmations, now is your time to say them. Alternatively, you can set reminders on your phone, rely on extreme accountability, or plaster a poster of your goal in a place you see it every day.

- **Step 5: Prioritize your goal**
Give more importance to your goal than anything else in your life. Come up with a plan and then use the ABC method to remain focused on the tasks needed to realize your vision.

- **Step 6: Baby steps**
Now it's time for action. So take a small step toward your goal. Maybe that's exercising for 20 minutes on Tuesday, or putting 50 bucks in savings this month. Whatever the target, with each small win you'll begin to build confidence. You will begin to believe.

Hey, hey, hey, hey, hey, hey..."Didn't you say there were 7 steps?"

Well, you caught me, dude. I most certainly did in this section's heading. But the last step is so important that it can't be summed up in a couple sentences. In fact, step 7 may be the only one some dudes need. What is it?

It all comes back to last chapter's core message: surround yourself with others who are chasing or have already accomplished your goal. The philosophy behind this step is why programs like Alcoholics Anonymous are so effective. Recovering alcoholics see group members breaking their alcohol dependency...and then the inkling of belief begins to grow, "What if I can do that, too?"

If you want to quit smoking but feel hopeless, try and find a group of dudes who've quit or are in the process of quitting, and spend as much time with them as possible. Being around positive influences will grow your confidence. This is what happened when I joined the writing community I mentioned in the last chapter. When I saw people succeeding in the community, I knew I could succeed, too. And when I posted questions in the forum, people were supportive of me, coaching me along, telling me I could become a full-time freelance writer. This had a tremendous effect on my confidence and my belief that I could do it.

No matter the habit you're changing, positive influences and support groups can inspire belief and stack the deck in your favor. To take this a step further, books and podcasts can also act as a support group. The voices of authorities can inspire belief and reveal the path to your goal. If you want to lose weight, then read books or listen to podcasts about weight loss for an hour every day. The more you flood your mind with the change you want to produce, the more you will believe. Sooner than you know it, the change will start to materialize in your life.

Wrestling with giants

Changing your habits is no easy task. Many of them are ingrained deep in our psyches and have been reinforced repeatedly over years, and sometimes decades. Reversing these patterns can seem like a monumental task.

You may try dozens of times and fail again, and again, and again....

After many failures, it can feel as though some higher power is laughing at you. Pushing you back down in the dirt just as you were getting up...crushing your confidence, spirits, and hope.

How can you believe when failure overwhelms you? When the light at the end of the tunnel is snuffed out and replaced by a cold, lifeless, blackness?

It may feel like you're gasping for air...but just take a minute.

Breathe, sit yourself down, and say the following two words. Big picture.

When you no longer see the light, you must imagine it. Right now your goal may only exist in your mind, but if you keep moving forward, then your defeat is only a temporary setback. Just remember, take baby steps and focus on the stairs. Not the staircase.

And guess what? You've already taken your first step. By completing this book, you're armed with the knowledge to change your habits, create a big-picture goal, and accomplish both.

Now just continue to take action.

That's where the next chapter comes in. Every tactic mentioned in this book is listed out and summarized for easy reference. So what are you waiting for?

Turn the page already, pick a few tactics, choose a new habit and go get em', dude.

Chapter 8

The habit cheat sheet: 23 tactics to make or break any habit

We've covered a lot of ground in this book. And now I want to make it as easy as possible for you to start or stop any habit at will, and accomplish the big goals you're chasing. Here's a list of all the habit-change tactics in this book, summarized:

1. Action triggers
Where and when will you perform your habit? In your apartment's gym at 11am? On your living room meditation cushion immediately after dinner? Visualize the exact time and location you'll complete your habit, and you'll easily remember to do it.

2. Write it down
Write your habit down in your planner, to-do list, or calendar. If you write it, you're more likely to accomplish it.

3. Track your habits
Tracking habits in a spreadsheet helps you gather data and stay focused. To learn if there's a correlation between your wins, losses and other

behavior, note these down in the sheet and reflect on your progress each week.

4. Perform your habit in the morning
In the morning, the call of the bar, your buddies, or your bed is less likely to tempt you away from your habit—unexpected events won't derail your efforts. You have full control over your mornings.

5. Habit stack
Leverage the power of your current habits to start a new one. Slot your new habit in between established habits.

6. Alter your environment
Change your surroundings to use less willpower. Remove the distractions, temptations, and people who habitually do the behavior you want to avoid, and it will be much easier to change your habit.

7. Replacement
Swap out your bad habit for something healthier. For example, replace cigarettes with gum, coffee with green smoothies, a cookie with some social interaction, or the like. Replace and thy urge will weaken.

8. Exercise your willpower muscles

Practice habit change regularly over a set period of days. Participate in Lent or block out a period of 30-60 days of your choosing to test new habits.

9. Expect failure

Mainly for the stubborn, excruciating habits. You will stumble, you will feel defeated—keep going. Failure is part of the process.

10. Mind your turbulent times

Pregnancy or the birth of a child can throw your world into disarray. A new job or flood of work can impact other parts of your life causing goals to fall by the wayside. If you're trying to start a habit during a big life change or personal crisis, realize your risk of failure has probably quadrupled.

11. Identify your kryptonite

Half the battle of winning the habit change game is understanding your core roadblock. Know your core weakness, and plan a strategy to sidestep the obstacle.

12. Extreme accountability

Put your money where your mouth is...or a nude picture of yourself (kidding on the last one). Have your buddy hold you accountable through public embarrassment, lost money, or doing something against your principles. Make failure painful.

13. Define a crystal clear goal
Make your goal measurable, concrete, specific, and within your control. Instead of a goal to "eat healthier", be clearer and say, "I will eat four cups of veggies a day and exercise for 30 minutes, four days a week—with the goal of losing 25 pounds by November 5."

14. Daily reminders
Set a daily reminder about your habit. Maybe that's simply a giant sign on your bedroom door that says, "Exercise, dude." Maybe it's a reminder on your phone every day that tells you to stop smoking. If the reminder is somewhat painful, like my dining room move, then your odds of success increase exponentially.

15. Prioritize
Use the ABC method to focus on the important things. Have competing priorities? Ask yourself, "Which task will make a bigger difference in my life?"

16. Find your *why*
Focus on the prize. When you achieve your goal, what exactly do you get? While your goal is the target, your *why* is the reward for winning. Maybe

that's the ability to quit your job, earn an income of $20,000 a month, or take a six-month backpacking trip through Europe. Whatever it is, your *why* is the motivational force that enables you to persevere when the going gets tough.

17. Big picture reminder
When you suffer a major setback, sit yourself down and say two words—big picture. Then remember your crystal clear goal, visualize your reward, and remind yourself there's something bigger you're chasing. Your failure today is only a temporary setback in the grand scheme of things.

18. Baby steps
Take action with one small step at a time. Instead of exercising six days a week from the get-go, start with one or two days, and build on that.

19. Surround yourself with cheerleaders
Not literally. But instead get around dudes who want to change the same habit as you and who are supportive. Surround yourself with positive influences.

20. Find a model
Someone who has already accomplished your desired habit change. Find out what that person did, and copy the behavior. Maybe you model the

behaviors outlined in a book, of an expert online, someone you know, or the dude staring back at you in the mirror.

21. Get a coach
If you want to level up your habit game, combine the last two tactics and hire a coach. Not only will you gain an experienced, positive influence who has been in your shoes, knows your struggles, and has conquered them, but you'll also have wasted money on the coach if you fail.

22. Join an online community
Similar to the last three tactics, learn from the successes of other community members and soak up the positive vibes of the group. What's more, seeing others like you succeed can instill in you the most important action you need to do in order to conquer your habit...

23. Believe
The foundation of everything. Without belief, you are your own obstacle. Don't just think you're great, know it. Keep your chin up, follow the steps above, and know in your core you can achieve whatever you put your mind to.

Also by the author

Written by an ordinary dude, for ordinary dudes, *An Ordinary Dude's Guide to Meditation* will unravel the perplexing rhetoric often associated with meditation, and speak to you straight.

Packed with **practical explanations** of meditation's **transformational power** and step-by-step **instructions on how to meditate**, *An Ordinary Dude's Guide to Meditation* is your first step to gain all the calm and clarity meditation has to offer.

Available at Amazon.com

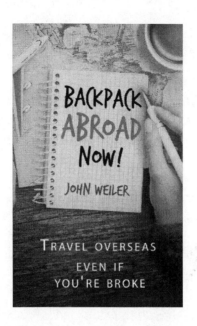

Dream of vagabonding the globe for months on end? Imagine the freedom. The adventure. The new experiences that will forever change your life. But first...how do you get abroad?

Backpack Abroad Now! will teach you how to plan your adventure, **one step at a time**. I saved up for an epic 11-month backpacking journey, while earning less than $17,000 a year, and have been living and traveling abroad for over 6 years and counting. This is the guide I wish I had before starting...when I was overwhelmed and broke, dreaming about traveling the world.

Available at Amazon.com

Special Thanks

An *Ordinary Dude's Guide to Habit* was not created by a single dude alone in his man cave while downing beers (though certainly a few beers were drunk). My beta readers provided some exceptional feedback that changed the structure of the book and pointed out some holes where more content was needed. So thank you to Kris Kristensen, Andy Hasdal, and Deb Craig Weiler. I know you all have busy lives, and it means the world to me that you take some time to read my quirky books and offer thoughtful feedback. You guys rock.

To my editors Cheyenne Hollis and Chris Wotton, thanks for your suggestions, speedy turnaround, and pointing out some of my idiotic grammar issues.

Of course, to my lovely dude (yes, ladies can be dudes, too) Arissara Suratanon. Thanks for putting up with the tumultuous lifestyle of a boyfriend who's a writer, my 6-day-a-week work schedule, and the nights where I down one beer too many and keep you awake with my multiple trips to the loo. With the exception of the latter, it will not always be this way.

Lastly, to my parents. Thank you for always believing in me, encouraging me to shoot for the moon, and for all the laughs along the way. This book wouldn't be here if it weren't for you.

Props *(aka Endnotes)*

INTRODUCTION

5   Investing as a metaphor. Darren Hardy. *The Compound Effect: Jumpstart Your Income, Your Life, Your Success* (New York: Vanguard Press, 2011), 40-41. In these particular pages, Hardy talks about how a cup of coffee a day can add up to $51,833.79 in twenty years.

CHAPTER 1

9   Thomas Edison failed a thousand times. Dr. Gary S. Goodman. "EXACTLY HOW MANY TIMES DID EDISON FAIL? Find Out for Yourself!" Nightingale-Conant,   http://www.nightingale.com/newsletters/556/ (accessed September 6, 2018). Well, dude. Complete transparency, it appears there's quite a debate about the number of Edison's failed attempts at the lightbulb. 1,000 seems like a popular number, but as this article explains, the real answer is uncertain. Let's just say he failed a lot.

CHAPTER 2

22 1996 study by Roy Baumeister. Chip Heath and Dan Heath. *Switch: How to Change Things When Change is Hard* (New York: Currency, 2010), 8-10. While the study is originally by Roy Baumeister, I came across it in *Switch*, which I based this telling on. For more information on this study, check out the article by Hans Villarica (April 9, 2012) "The Chocolate-and-Radish Experiment That Birthed the Modern Conception of Willpower," *The Atlantic*, https://www.theatlantic.com/health/archive/2012/04/the-chocolate-and-radish-experiment-that-birthed-the-modern-conception-of-willpower/255544/ (accessed September 6, 2018)

34 A style of habit change. Leo Babauta. *The Power of Less: The Fine Art of Limiting Yourself to the Essential...in Business and in Life* (New York: Hachette Books, 2009), 33-36

CHAPTER 3

45 ABC prioritization method. Brian Tracy. *Eat That Frog!: 21 Great Ways to Stop Procrastinating and Get More Done in Less Time* (San Francisco: Berrett-Koehler Publishers, 2007), 37-40

51 Action trigger. Heath. *Switch*, 209-212

57 Forrester analyst once estimated. JP Mangalindan (February 3, 2015) "Inside Amazon Prime," *Fortune*, http://fortune.com/2015/02/03/inside-amazon-prime/ (accessed September 6, 2018)

57   **Bezos believed in the service**. Brad Stone. *The Everything Store: Jeff Bezos and the Age of Amazon* (New York: Back Bay Books, 2013), 188

57   **Setbacks as temporary**. Stone. *The Everything Store*, 159. While seeing setbacks as temporary is mentioned on this page, this theme is illustrated throughout the book through various stories.

CHAPTER 4

70   **Stop a bad habit**. Charles Duhigg. *The Power of Habit: Why We do What We do and How to Change* (London: Random House Books, 2013), 61-78

CHAPTER 5

83   **Getting a cookie every day**. Duhigg. *The Power of Habit*, 277-80, 283, 285

Made in the USA
Lexington, KY
22 December 2018